I0202178

Stormy

Skies

Mbali Madaki

Stormy Skies Copyright © 2015 by Mbali Madaki.

All rights reserved. Printed in the United States of America. No part of this book may be used or reproduced in any manner whatsoever without written permission except in the case of brief quotations embodied in critical articles or reviews.

This book is semi-non-fictional and semi-autobiographical. However, names, characters, businesses, organizations, places, events and incidents either are the product of the author's imagination or are used fictitiously. Any resemblance to actual persons, living or dead, events, or locales is entirely coincidental.

For information contact: info@uptownmediaventures.com

Book and Cover design by Team Uptown

ISBN: 978-1-68121-021-6

First Edition: June 2015

10 9 8 7 6 5 4 3 2 1

This book is dedicated to my mom, father, sisters, neighbors, the people of South Africa, and anyone who has dreams that survive the storms of life

Page left intentionally blank

Chapters   Page

Introduction

I wrote *Stormy Skies*, hoping to educate people, young or old, that it doesn't matter where you come from; who your parents are; whether you are a cheese girl or not; whether you are ugly or beautiful - you can be anything you want to be in life! If you put your mind to it you can do it. Those who are laughing at you while you are busy trying to achieve your dream may wish to be you later. This book is semi-autobiographical.

I grew up wishing to be my sister Julia. I thought I was ugly, but when I grew up people started to tell me that I really was beautiful and must be a model. In my late teens I started to gain confidence and to have dreams, wishing to be educated. My mother and my sisters cannot believe that I wrote a book, but they are so proud of me. People from my community are asking me questions about how did I write my first book. I am happy to know that *Stormy Skies* is going to deliver the message of self-determination and faith to the people of my community.

Chapter 1

Crossroads

The following experiences are mine – most people call me Portia. My given name is Mbali Madaki. I was born in 1984, in Cape Town at Crossroads, South Africa. I'm the second born of the children. My older sister's name is Julia. Our mother is Elizabeth and our father is Eric.

Our family's faith was Christian. We attended the Old Apostolic Church. My father, Eric, worked at a hospital as a public worker and my mother, Elizabeth, was a house wife. My mother really loved my father.

My sister Julia looked like our father, but I did not look like my parents. No one could tell who I looked like. I could not either, but never really thought about it. My parents always said that I looked like my aunt who was in Transkei.

Julia was seven years old and I was three years old when I could remember things. At that time I did not realize anything bad because I was young. My parents used to talk sweet things about my sister Julia.

"Julia is gonna make it in life, she beautiful, smart and is intelligent," they would always say.

They tended to laugh and be dismissive of me. My mother would always make Julia beautiful. She would make her hair nicely, buying her nice dresses and Julia always looked like a princess.

My parents would buy trousers for me and made me a wear a boy's haircut.

They would always say "Portia is looking like a boy. "

They acted like they believed that I was ugly and girl clothes would not suit me. I did not mind because I wanted my father to love me like he loved my sister Julia. Because of this I acted like a boy because I noticed that my father really wished to have a boy.

I was having trouble with a broken shoulder. My right arm worked funny but no told me who broke my arm. My parents promised to take me to a hospital when I became 16 years old to fix my arm. I kept asking to get my arm fixed, but they all would just laugh at me.

No one told HEQG who broke my arm...

Chapter 2
Transkei

I was five years old and Julia was nine years old when our mother, Elizabeth, became pregnant. At the end of the month my father, Eric, decided that the family must go to Transkei to visit his father. My grandfather's name was Tiger because he was old and had long strong nails. Oh, I forgot to tell you that they are Xhosa people.

They decided to go on a Friday of that week. On Thursday Elizabeth was busy preparing food for the way and packed everyone's clothes. Eric took five days off from his work. On Friday the family caught a bus and arrived at Transkei on Saturday.

We stayed there nicely until Tiger told my parents that Julia was going to stay with him. Julia was so very happy, but Elizabeth was so very worried.

"You are going to be left alone with your grandfather," Elizabeth told Julia.

Elizabeth did not want to leave Julia but she had to follow the culture. The Xhosa culture required respecting your in-laws and to do as they said. The family returned to Cape Town without Julia. My parents began to treat me like Julia. I was so happy with the change even though my mother was worried about Julia.

My mother was worried because Transkei was the rural area and there was no electric or water. People had to fetch wood and water in the mountain.

In Cape Town, at that time, the white people did not want the black people there. They were burning the houses of black people at night. One night Elizabeth heard a knock on the door. She asked my father Eric to open the door.

He was shocked to find five white soldiers telling him to "get out!"

They wanted to burn our house down.

Chapter 3

Soldiers

When Elizabeth heard the soldiers she just took one blanket and cover for me. My father held me tight. The soldiers told them to go quickly but my father requested to pack some of the things they would need in the house. The soldiers refused and told them to go as fast as they could.

I told my mother to take my doll that was on the floor.

"We will come tomorrow to take the doll," my mother said.

We went to the bush to sleep there. When we arrived we found 60 or more people who were having the same problem as we were. Everyone seemed to have a different reaction. Some were crying like we were, others were laughing, and others were singing.

I was worried about my doll.

In the middle of the night, a group of soldiers came to the bush and gave the people blankets and plastic to use it as a bed. Some of the men decided to take the plastic, make a big plastic house, share the blankets, and sleep in groups.

At that time black people were helping each other. In the morning Eric was supposed to go to work but he did not because he did not have clothes to change and a place to wash. All the people were hoping to find something in their houses, so they decided to go and check their homes.

Elizabeth went with Eric and they asked a woman to look after me.

"Don't forget my doll and her red suit!" I told my mother.

All the people laughed when they heard me saying that.

Chapter 4

A Night in the Bush

Elizabeth was shocked to find her house totally burnt. She could not find anything - not even my doll! My mother started crying and my father was crying too. They were hungry and worried about me. My father held my mother and told her that everything was going to be fine. Eric took a big stone and told Elizabeth to sit and wait for him. She sat and waited for him.

Crossroads was dirty. People were throwing rubbish everywhere, but that really helped Eric that day. Eric found a dirty plastic container and washed it. He collected orange covers, washed them nicely, and looked for a two liter bottle. He washed it nicely and filled it with water. He took it to Elizabeth and begged her to eat.

Elizabeth started to eat small amounts until she discovered the orange covers were not bad. She ate with my father and they drank the water. They kept some of orange covers for me.

The time was past noon during the day. They went to the bush and found me playing outside of that plastic house. They took me in and sat in the corner.

"Is the house burnt?" I asked.

"What did you find in the house?"

"What does the house look like now?"

They told me the truth about everything. My father took one orange cover and ate it.

"Mmmh that's nice," he said.

I took one and started eating. My parents smiled and gave me water to drink.

Eric and some other men were collecting drums. Other men where cutting trees. They used the tree stalks and drums to build a shelter for each person who lost their house. They named the bush the "New Crossroads."

After 6 pm that day people from a church called "Roma" came with bread and soup for people. They brought track suits for the children and "tackies." They were white ladies. That day I received a black and grey track suit and black and white tackies.

Chapter 5

Father Goes Back to Work

Elizabeth and Eric were happy to have a shelter now. Elizabeth advised Eric to go to work the next day. He agreed. They slept without taking a bath. Eric woke up early in the morning and left Elizabeth sleeping. He used a shoe lace to keep the door closed.

He went to the job early because he did not have the money to buy a train ticket. He arrived at his job so early that he had to sit at the gate with the security. He was waiting for the 6 a.m. opening time for the hospital. It was 4:30 in the morning and he waited until he fell asleep. While he was sleeping he heard someone calling his name. When he opened his eyes he found Dr. Smith standing in front of him.

Dr. Smith asked him to come with him to his office. They went into the office and sat down.

"Where were you yesterday and why didn't you come to work?" Dr. Smith asked my father.

"Why aren't you wearing your uniform today?"

My father told Dr. Smith everything. Dr. Smith was worried and promised to help him. Dr. Smith called his wife. Afterwards, he apologized to Eric.

"I can't help you the way I like," Dr. Smith told my father.

Dr. Smith then cancelled his appointments and told Eric that he wanted to see his new shelter.

"We must go there now!" said Dr. Smith.

When they arrived there they found Elizabeth sitting down holding me. Dr. Smith introduced himself to my mother. My mother returned a greeting while she brushed my hair. Dr. Smith then asked my parents to go with him into town.

Dr. Smith took them to a "Shoprite" store and they took a trolley. Then Dr. Smith brought a big basin for washing, towels, soap, "Colgate" tooth paste, a roll on, flame for cooking, and groceries including chips, chocolate, and juice for me. He then gave my father 500 rand to give to my mother to buy the things that they might really need.

My mother went to the "Pepstore" and bought panties for her and me. She also bought a bra for herself along with two dresses for herself and me. She bought some shoes, and then the money was gone.

We went to Dr. Smith's car that was outside the "Pepstore." On the way home my father asked Dr. Smith to stop in the garage - he wanted to buy paraffin. Dr. Smith stopped at the garage and a man called Norman bought the paraffin.

We went to the shelter. After we arrived at the shelter, they took the stuff in. Dr. Smith said that he would be back after an hour. Everyone thanked him and he left. They put the paraffin in boiling water that was over a flame to wash, cook, and eat. My father asked everyone to stand up and pray and thank God for meeting nice white men like Dr. Smith. Everybody stood up and prayed.

Chapter 6

My First School

After finishing their prayer, everyone stayed nicely in their shelter. After an hour Dr. Smith came with a big caravan. He told everyone to use the caravan like the house while they don't have a house. He told my father to be at work the next day and gave him 200 rand to use for transport.

Everyone stayed nicely at "New Crossroads" although the soldiers used to come and spread the "tea gas" for fun. Black people had a plan though - they would take wet cloth and cover their nose or others would put "Vaseline" in their nose until the tea gas smell finished. After three years my father found a house at Khayelitsha in Cape Town. The house had two rooms and had a toilet inside. I was seven, turning 8 years old that year. I never went to school before. In Khayelitsha there was a new school that was called "k1." My mother went there to register me. The school fees were 5 rand and I was accepted at the school.

They said that I could start on Monday and my mother was so happy. Saturday my father went to town to buy a new uniform, books, pencils, and crayons. I was so happy to have a uniform and I could not wait for Monday!

On Sunday we went to church. Monday my mother prepared my father to go to work and then she woke me up. She washed me up nicely, made my hair nicely, and dressed me for school. After I had my school uniform on, before we were about to leave for school, I ran into the room and stood in front of a mirror and smiled.

My mother took me to school and I met my teacher. My teacher showed me where I was going to sit. My mother went into the class and my teacher asked the children to introduce themselves and to tell her what they wanted to be when they grew up.

The children introduced themselves and told their dreams.

When it was my turn I stood up and said, "my name is Portia, I want to be a president."

"You can't want to become a president - people have to vote for you," said my teacher.

Then I thought and said "I want to be a soldier."

All the children laughed and I sat down and wondered why the people were laughing.

Chapter 7

Julia Returns

I studied well at "k1." My sister Julia was back from Transkei. By this time, my mother had another child who was five years old at that time. Her name is Patricia. She looked like my father, Eric, and she was the favorite girl because she was young. Julia was older so my mother used to say she first saw that she could give birth to a child with Julia that is why they like her.

There was a man who liked to come to visit my mother. This guy would come to my house and asked my mother questions about me. When he did this my mother would tell me to take this man half way and then this man would give me 10 rand. He would tell me he was going to come next week. I did not know this man so I did not care about him. I was just 10 years old at that time.

The man kept on coming over until my sister Julia began to suspect something. One day, when the man came over, Julia started crying.

"Why does this guy look like Portia?" said Julia.

My mother shouted to the man saying "I told you not to come here; people are going to suspect something!"

"I want my child Elizabeth," the man said.

"You don't have a child here!"

Julia began to cry again and said "I'm going to tell my father."

The man took 20 rand out of his pocket and gave it to me.

"I'm gonna come and take you my child. I want to fix your arm," the man told me.

I just looked at him. I saw that this man really did look like me and prepared myself to go to school.

On the way to school Julia told me that this man was my father. I was worried that I would lose my family.

"If that man is my father are we still sisters?" I asked Julia.

"No - you are not my sister. We just share a mother. My sister is Patricia. You can see that we look alike," said Julia.

I started crying.

Chapter 8

No Where to Go

My life really changed. I felt so alone. I started to see the rejection from my mother. I wished to be Eric's child. I would to do things to please him, be obedient, and listen to him. But Eric would only notice bad things.

Julia used to beat me and hide my food. She would call me names. When I would talk back to Julia, my parents would always take Julia's side. They continued to treat me that way until I learned how to stand up for myself.

By this time I was 15 years old and Julia was 19 years old. One day I was coming in from school and put my bag into the room. Julia threw my school bag outside. I became angry.

"Ma you see what Julia is doing?"

"Leave me alone Portia," my mother would say.

I took out my school blazer and went straight to Julia, who was sitting down in a chair.

"Bring back my books please Julia," I said.

"Please don't make me laugh," Julia said, laughing.

I pushed Julia and she fell down with the chair. Then I slapped Julia in her face. Before I could realize I was on the floor after my mother pushed me. I stood back up.

"Say you are not my mother!"

"I'm not your mother so get out of my house Portia!"

"I will be out and I promise I will never come back!" I said.

I packed my clothes in a big bag. When I was done I said "goodbye" to my mother.

"Bye bye and pass my greetings to where you are going," my mother said.

Julia laughed at me.

I left with my school uniform carrying my big bag and the school bag to town. I did not know where I was going. I decided to sit down at Cape Town and watch people until it got dark.

Chapter 9

Unexpected Angel

I was tall, slender, light in complexion, with a long natural hair. Old women really liked me. I stood at the station until it started to rain. I wanted to die that day. There were people who were asking me questions, but I did not reply until this handsome boy, who was so clean, wearing nice clothes, came by.

"I'm staying there. I passed here five times just to check if you were still here," he said.

He introduced himself and asked me my name. I told him and he asked me to trust him. I looked him in the eye. He had a begging eye so I agreed to go with this guy, "Thabo," who was 22 years old. He was the manager of "Jet Store" staying in a bachelor flat.

He gave me his shorts, a T-shirt, a big white towel, and some things to wash and shower myself in the bathroom. I washed and wore the shorts and the T-shirt. I combed my hair and came out of the bathroom.

"You are so beautiful my dear Portia," he said.

I became scared.

"Don't be scared. I have my girlfriend staying downstairs. I can go sleep with her if you are not going to be scared," he said.

He gave me food and I ate. I went to wash the plate.

Thabo said "I don't want to hear your story now but when you are comfortable you will tell me. Now I will help you and stay with you. I want you to pass matric tomorrow. Please don't go to school. I want to take you somewhere."

I agreed and slept in a bed while he slept on the floor. In the morning he went to his work. Around 12 noon, he came back finding me washing my clothes.

"Wash the clothes quickly and see what I brought for you!" he said.

"Close your eyes."

I did not close my eyes but he gave me a plastic "jet" bag. Inside there was a pink dress, white shoes, and white earrings.

"Wash and wear that dress. I want to take you to my job for shopping. I have a discount there."

I washed and wore the dress with the shoes and the earrings and looked in the mirror.

"Thank you Lord!" I said.

Chapter 10

First Love

Thabo and I became lovers because I noticed that Thabo really loved me and he treated me nicely. He did everything for me, helping me when I did my school work. I was very good at school.

My mother did not look for me for three years.

Thabo would go to visit his parents and left me in his flat. When I turned 18 years old, I still lived with Thabo. I was in grade 12.

Thabo bought me a nice black and gold dress and the gold for my matric dance. Thabo was my partner in my matric dance. We were driving Thabo's new car when we were going to the matric dance.

I saw Julia and her four friends standing next to the gate. We stopped the car and I got out quickly and held Thabo's hand. Julia did not recognize me.

"Hey ladies look at that beautiful girl. I like her shoes," this loud voice said.

I passed them and said "hello Julia."

"Portia listen," she said.

I just went and entered the hall and enjoyed my matric dance with my handsome Thabo.

After two weeks I was in class writing a final exam. The teacher told me that when I finished writing that I must come and take something from her.

After I finished writing, I went to the teacher. She gave me a letter. I put it in my bag and went to Thabo's flat. When I arrived, I sat down and read the letter.

"Dear Portia, I really need to see you. I'm in trouble my child. Please come back home. I really miss you and I want to talk to you, please my child. From your father Eric"

Chapter 11

The Letter

I was happy to receive a letter but was also angry because I started to stay with a guy and lost my virginity when I was 15 years old. I was blaming my family for that although I was thanking them because I was happy to be with Thabo.

I took off my school uniform, washed myself, put lotion on my body, put on my make-up, put on my yellow dress and yellow shoes and put on my perfume. When I finished I cleaned the flat, cooked, and watched the TV.

Thabo came from work, kissed me and asked me about my day. I told him everything and Thabo was really shocked to hear about the letter and begged me to go and see Eric. That night he even offered to take me in his car. I agreed and put on my white earrings and fixed my make up and left with Thabo.

On the way I made a silent prayer. I was so scared. We were so quiet in the car. We found my family's home dark, like there was no one inside. We got out of the car and knocked. We were shocked to hear someone ask: "who is that, Portia?"

"It's me," I said.

My mother opened the door, she saw me and screamed!

"Oh my baby you old now!" she said.

My mother hugged me.

"Can we come in?" I asked.

"Yes my baby, you can come. Also my son, you can sit there."

My mother showed Thabo a place to sit. Julia said "I told you mama she's beautiful."

"Yes, she is," my mother said.

My mother entered the room with me. I just stood there in the room and looked in. Eric, my father, was sitting in a bed with his legs covered with a blanket. He looked at me. He was so slender.

"Do you see Portia?" my mother said.

"I do," my father said.

"Come stand in front of me. I want to talk to you."

Wearing my yellow dress, I told him everything about my day.

Chapter 12

Visit to Khayelitsha

I was looking at my father, Eric. While he was busy talking old good things about me, I was thinking that no matter what happens - Eric is my father. I just smiled and gave him a big hug and told him to get well. I told him that I would come and see him. I told my parents about Thabo and how he helped me.

They thanked Thabo. My parents told me not to worry about my father because he was just having a "tb" and he would be fine.

Thabo gave them 300 rand for electric and told them that everything was going to be alright. I hugged my mother and told her that I wished them well.

Julia was just smiling.

Thabo and I went to our place and slept peaceful that night. After a month I got my matric. I made it with high marks!

My mother found a job as a domestic worker. My father was fine and was working again. Julia was dating another boy. His name was Vickie. I traveled by train when I visited my parents.

In South Africa, since Mandela became president in 1994 education was free. People did not want to go to school so it was hard for them to get a job because Mandela came with the law that people must have a matric to get a job except the domestic workers and the garden boys. Because of this crime was high. Murders and robberies were increasing and people where heartless.

Chapter 13

Goodbye Cape Town

People had freedom now. They stopped fighting with white people, but now they were using their freedom in a bad way. Some were putting candles into their children, lying to social workers saying their father raped them so that they could get new houses. Others would burn their shelters so that they could get a new house and new furniture from the government.

There was too much robbery, gangsters, and rape. People were not safe in their own houses. The police did not care about the safety of the people, so my father decided to leave Cape Town and go to stay on a farm called Vredendal. He went to Vredendal to look for a job. Luckily he found one and came back with a big truck that was driven by the owner of the farm. His name was Peter.

My father told my mother that they must pack their stuff because they going to stay at Vredendal. My mother called and told me to come to their place with my stuff because they were going to stay in Vredendal. I told them that they could go and I would come and visit them during school holidays.

I was studying at Cape College studying human and social development. I was singing and dancing too. My father, mother, Julia and Patricia went to Vredendal.

Peter, the owner of the farm, told them that my father was going to be security on the farm. My mother was going to work at the dairy. Julia was going to work on the farm and Patricia was going to study there. Peter had a school on his farm.

Peter gave them a four room house that had a shower. Peter told them that they were going to get maize meals and milk for free and on Wednesdays he was going to give them bread, chicken, and butter. He said he paid his workers 250 rand every Friday.

They were happy. It was at night when they arrived so they cooked, ate, washed, and slept. In the morning they when went to work they were surprised to see that all the people that were drinking alcohol too much. Even the young children were smoking and drinking. The young people were not studying - they working on the farm, but they were the nicest people although they did not have dreams.

Chapter 14

Finding a Friend

I enjoyed studying at Cape College. I was happy to have Thabo because he was doing everything for me. I found a friend at school, her name was Alma. Alma was a beautiful young brilliant girl at school. She wanted to be a social worker.

We would go shopping after school. Alma always had money telling me that she had a "rich uncle." We would go to stay at Thabo's flat, eat, listen to music, and dance. Alma would receive a call and tell me that someone wanted to see her.

"I will be back," she would say.

Then she would be back after an hour or two with something new or money. Ladies in my class told me to stop going with Alma because Alma was not a "right person." I did not understand them and continued being friends with Alma.

One Saturday I was going to shop and saw Alma standing on the corner. We were happy to see each other, talked, and laughed.

"We will see each other Monday," we both told each other.

I went to buy a cold drink and went to the flat. I stayed with Thabo nicely until we slept. In the morning I heard a knock. The person was knocking fast. I ran to the door asking "who is it?"

"It's me!" the lady said.

I opened the door and this girl, wearing a short skirt, was there.

"Your friend Alma is dead. She was killed yesterday by a white man who kills black prostitutes. He cut almas head and left Alma there with no clothes!" she excitedly told me.

Chapter 15

Alma's Disappearance

I was shocked and asked the girl if she was joking.

"No," she said.

My brain stopped working for a while, and then I heard Thabo.

"What's going on Portia?" Thabo asked.

"They cut my friend's head thinking that she's a prostitute," I said.

"Are you talking about Alma Portia?"

"Yes, the girl said Alma was a prostitute. She asked saying 'and you not a prostitute?'"

"I told her that I am not a prostitute! And how did this happen?"

The girl said most of the black prostitutes knew about this guy, a white guy, but he could speak Xhosa.

"I guess Alma did not know the guy," said the girl.

"When did this happen?" Thabo asked.

"Come with me and I will tell you when we are going," the girl said.

Thabo took his car keys we went with our sleeping clothes in the car.

"They tried to stop Alma but everything happened fast so this morning. When that white guy came, the secretary noticed that the guy was nervous and red in his face. When the secretary tried to talk to him, he just ran. So when the secretary went to the room he booked she found Almas head in the door and the body in the door. Then the poor girl started crying," the girl told Thabo and me.

When we arrived at the guest house we stopped and looked watching the police and ambulance. We saw Almas body covered with a black bag and put into a vehicle. There was an old black man who was crying.

Thabo asked the girl "can I take you home?"

"I would love that," the girl said.

We took the girl to her home and Thabo went to the shop and bought sleeping tablets for me. When we arrived to our flat we washed ourselves, ate, took sleeping tablets, and went to sleep.

Monday I went to school at the college. They put Almas photo up with "rest in peace" written in every corner. I was standing watching Almas photo wondering why my friend became a prostitute. Then I heard four girls laughing. I looked at them and one of them said, "Why is this prostitute looking at us?"

CHAPTER 16

A Life Changing Phone Call

I watched those girls and then I went to my class. In class students were talking about Alma. I sat at my desk. Some of the students went to me asking me questions about Alma's death.

"Is it true that you were with Alma the day Alma died?" some asked me.

I did not answer them. The teacher came in the class, greeted everyone nicely and started talking about Alma's death. I became bored, left school and went to Thabo's flat. When I arrived at the flat I sat down and took out my cellphone. I looked at my gallery and I saw Alma's photo there.

I thought that maybe people were mistaken and maybe Alma was not dead. I decided to call Alma's phone number. I called and the phone rang. When I heard the phone ring I just dropped the call and jumped saying "yes!"

I then decided to change clothes and eat. I wore Thabo's shorts and T-shirt. After I finished I took my phone and called Alma. Then phone rang twice.

"Hello," someone answered.

"Hey Alma where are you?" I said.

"Sorry who am I talking with?" the woman said.

"I'm Portia."

"Oh Portia, we heard a lot about you, you must please come and see us tomorrow, I'm Alma's mother," the woman said.

I promised to come and asked the woman to send the address.

"To this number?"

"Yes," I said.

"Goodbye Portia, I will see you tomorrow."

"Goodbye mama," I said.

Chapter 17

A Visit to Alma's Place

Later that day I told Thabo about my day. I told him about the call I made to Alma, and about how I felt when Alma's phone rang. I told Thabo that I was glad that I made that call because now I would be able to go to Alma's burial.

"How are you going to go there?" Thabo asked.

"I'm waiting for Alma's mother to send me the address."

Thabo bought take aways and we washed, ate and slept. In the morning Thabo left and went to his job. I decided not to go to school - I just wanted to be at home. When I woke up, I washed, brushed my teeth and wore my night dress. I started cleaning the flat. When I was about to finish cleaning I received a message from Alma's mother. She gave me her address to her house and said that she's waiting for me.

I was so happy and finished cleaning the house. I washed again, put on my summer dress, flat shoes, put on my jewelry, combed my hair and put make up on my face. I took my money and my cell phone; locked the flat and went to the taxi rank.

I caught the taxi that went to Gugulethu. I told the driver to take me off at section two. When the driver arrived at section two, the driver told me and I got out.

"Hide your phone because the gangsters are going to take it," the driver told me.

I thanked the driver and paid. While I waited for the change I came close to the taxi and quickly put my phone in my underwear. The driver gave me the change and asked "where is the phone little girl?"

I smiled and asked "little driver little?" The driver laughed and left. I stood there and checked the number. I saw that the house was very far because they were having a big tent. I quickly went there. At the gate of the house I found a woman standing. I asked the woman where I could find Alma's mother.

The women took me to the room.

"Miriam look who's here!" said the woman.

Miriam looked at me for a very long time.

"Are you Portia?"

I shook my head and Miriam hugged me and cried.

"Oh Portia, why you look like my baby?"

CHAPTER 18

A Father I Never Knew

I just stood there and watched Alma's mother crying. Miriam noticed that I was worried and told some women to take me to the sitting room. A TV was on and I watched as I sat in a big chair. A woman brought me a cold drink, biscuits and two glasses. She poured a cold drink for me and one for herself.

"I'm Nomathemba, Alma's aunt. We are so happy to see you but the problem is you really look like Alma. That is why Miriam has been crying. You remind her of Alma," the woman said to me.

"I understand, but I am really worried about her," I said.

"Please feel at home and do as you please like home," said Nomathemba.

I thanked Nomathemba and she went to the kitchen. I took my phone out of my underwear and called Thabo. The phone rang once and Thabo picked it up.

"You must come and fetch me at Alma's house," I said.

I gave Thabo the address of Alma's home then we hung up. After two hours I was sitting there and Nomathemba took me to a room and left me with Miriam, an old man, and two boys. They were all looking at me in a scary way.

I wanted to run.

"Where did you grow up little girl?" the man asked.

"I grew up at Khayelitsha," I responded.

"What is your mother's name?"

"My mama's name is Elizabeth," I said.

The man just stood up and felt my right shoulder.

"Oh my God! This is my baby! I am that man who used to visit you when you were young and gave you 20 rand the last time."

CHAPTER 19

A New Doll

The man said "I'm Thozama. I'm your real father. The first time I told you, you were too young to understand."

Then he hugged me and cried. He told me in my ears that it had been five years since the last time he bought me clothes because it was winter. He said he went to see my mother, Elizabeth, who took the clothes and threw them outside.

He told me that my mother said "you have a street kid in town," and he went in town to find his child. He said he asked people but the problem was that he did not have a current photo of me.

"Since that day I have been praying to God to protect you and dreamed about you. I'm so sorry my child," he said.

"I should have stole you when you were young but I'm happy now that you are here."

I was crying by this time.

"You see that woman is your mother now and these two boys are your brothers, the tall older one is Patrick and the short younger one is Andrew," he said.

"Then there is Alma and you, but Alma is two month older than you, so you are my little child."

Miriam said, "I asked Elizabeth to give me you when you were young but she did not want to."

I was tired of standing and just sat down next to the door and cried. Thozama quickly stood up and picked me up. He put me into the bed and Miriam covered me with a clean blanket and whispered to Thozama.

I was crying and Miriam was playing with my afro hair until I fell asleep. I slept for four hours. When I started to open my eyes I saw Thozama standing watching me with Miriam.

"Surprise!" they said.

Thozama then gave me a nice big new doll.

"Do you see this doll? It looks like the doll I bought you when you were young. I know you are

19 now but you will always be my baby girl," he said.

Thozama gave me a plastic container that had chocolate, chips, sweets, muffins, peanuts, cold drink, and biltongs. I smiled and went to the bathroom to wash my mouth. I took the doll and took all that stuff Thozama bought me to the sitting room. I sat down looking at the doll and smiled. I named the doll Alma and started eating my chocolate while watching TV.

CHAPTER 20
Mystery Father

Thozama came to me in the sitting room

"Can I sit next to you?" he said.

I nodded in the affirmative. Thozama then sat next to Me.

"My girl you are still young to stay with a man. But I don't blame you because you were not having a choice because no one was there for you. So I understand my girl. Don't take me wrong - daddy understands and I respect your boyfriend for looking after you and making you a beautiful girl and taking you to school," he said.

"But I'm doing what a father is supposed to do. My culture doesn't allow that to happen. What do you think my little girl?"

"I'm worried about Thabo. We've been staying together for a very longtime. He is my left brain.

He knows everything about me. He picked me up when I was down - I owe him my life," I said.

"He really loves me and I don't know how he is gonna feel about me staying with you. I think I must stay with you just to not compromise your culture."

"Don't worry my child. Everything is going to be fine. Just wear your shoes and follow me."

I wore the shoes and followed Thozama. Thozama went to Miriam and told her that we were "going now." He took the car keys, and I ran to the sitting room and took a packet of chips, a cold drink and my doll.

I was so happy, sitting in the front sit of the car. I looked at for a very long time at Thozama. He was quiet and driving.

"Are you really my father?" I asked. Thozama laughed.

"Yes, my girl. With all my children you are the one who really looks like me Portia," Thozama nodded while showed me his teeth.

"Do see my teeth look like yours, my lips, nose, your eyes and the color of your eyes. They look just like mine but I'm a man!" We both laughed.

I sent Thabo a message telling him to go quickly to the flat because I was coming with my father. I told him not to phone. When we arrived to the flat we found Thabo sitting there looking nervous. Thozama greeted Thabo and Thabo greeted Thozama back. Thabo was just shocked and looked at Thozama because he was expecting to see Eric.

CHAPTER 21

New Father – New Life

Thabo offered Thozama a place to sit. He asked him if he wanted anything to drink.

"I would love to have a glass of water," said Thozama.

I did not want to see Thabo hurt so I decided to take my doll to the bathroom and bath with my doll. I was now talking with the doll.

Thabo brought Thozama a glass of cold water. Thozama introduced himself to Thabo. Thozama told Thabo how hurt he felt for Alma's death and how happy he was for finding me.

"I don't know why Alma was selling her body because I was doing everything for Alma," Thozama said.

"Maybe I was not close enough to Alma," said Thozama as he started to cry.

"Why did Alma die like that?"

Thabo was really worried and nodded to everything Thozama was saying. He acted like he did not see that Thozama was crying. Thozama drank the water and wiped his tears.

"My boy I came here to thank you for looking after Portia nicely, taking her to school, feeding her, and buying her clothes. I really respect you for that."

"If it was not because of my culture I was going to let Portia stay with you but I can't because I'm a black man, so now I have come to tell you that I'm taking Portia home. That means I'm going back home with Portia."

Thabo started crying.

"I can't live without Portia. She's my soulmate," said Thabo.

"I'm not saying that you must breakup. You can come and visit and Portia can visit too," said Thozama.

Thabo begged Thozama to leave me there.

"I am going to bring Portia in my car," Thabo promised.

"Now we have to pack Portia clothes so we will follow later."

Thozama agreed and shouted telling me that he was going to see me later.

"Ok," I said.

After Thozama departed, I wrapped myself and went to Thabo. Thabo just looked at me and kissed me. I kissed him back. Thabo pushed me to the bed while he kissed me and quickly took off his clothes. We made love. After we were done, we talked, joked, and laughed.

I slept in Thabo's arms while he kissed me. At 10 o'clock p.m. I heard my phone ring. I looked and saw that it was Thozama,

I looked at Thabo. "What must I say now?"

CHAPTER 22

Commitment

Thabo told me to tell Thozama that we are coming.

"Hello my father," I said as I picked up the phone.

"Hi, are you still coming Portia?" He said.

"Yes daddy, we are coming," I said.

"Why do you sound like you are home Portia?"

"We are in the garage," I said.

"Ok my girl, I will be waiting for you."

"Ok daddy bye."

"Bye."

Thabo woke up and went straight to the wall drop taking my clothes out of the wall drop. He packed them into a big bag. I laughed.

"Why are you laughing Portia?" Thabo said.

"Because you are packing my clothes while you are not wearing anything!"

Thabo laughed and took a towel and wrapped himself. He continued to pack my clothes. When he finished he told me to go to wash and wear so that we could go. I started to cry.

Thabo sat next to me.

"What's wrong baby?"

I did not talk. I just stood up and went to the shower and washed. Thabo joined me and we started kissing.

"I want you Thabo," I said.

"Really Portia?" he said.

"Yes."

I acted like someone who really wanted it. We went to the bed and made love. When we were done I acted like someone who was pregnant. I just ran to the toilet and acted like I wanted to vomit. I changed and said my stomach was painful.

I asked Thabo to hold my in the stomach. Thabo was so happy to be a father and held my stomach the whole night. In the morning Thabo woke up slowly because he did not want to wake me up. I acted like I was sleeping because I did not want Thabo to take me to Gugulethu.

Thabo washed and put on his clothes. He took his wallet, car keys, and cellphone and left. I woke up and made the bed, washed, and went to school.

As I was entering my class Thabo called.

"Where are you Portia?"

"I'm at school."

"I'm with your father," Thabo said as he approached the school gate.

"Don't forget your books Portia."

I dropped my phone and walked slowly to the gate. As I got closer I noticed that Thabo was alone in the car. I started walking faster and entered into the car. I looked at Thabo with sad eyes.

Thabo squeezed my hand and drove away. We went to Thabo's flat and played a romantic movie.

"Sit next to me Portia," said Thabo.

I sat next to him. Thabo put his hand into his pocket and took out a box of jewelry. I opened it. I was shocked to see a gold diamond ring. Thabo put the ring on my finger.

"With this I promise to marry you."

Chapter 23

Captured by Culture

I really loved the ring. The ring made me love Thabo more. I just listened to Thabo while he was promising to marry me. I just looked at Thabo and gave him the biggest kiss ever.

"Take me to the mall and you are gonna pay for everything!" I laughed.

Thabo just nodded. I stood up and went to change my clothes because it was hot and what I was wearing was warm. I put on my white short dress, white pumpers (shoes), my jewelry, my perfume, and I put on some makeup. I made my afro shine, then I took my cellphone, eye brow pencil, lip stick, mirror, and my wallet and put them in my small bag.

"We can go now Mr. Thabo Mathlala," I said.

"Wow! You look nice my love. Just stand there - I want to take you a picture."

Thabo took his phone and told me to pose. I gladly posed and Thabo took my picture. He showed the picture and then we held each other's hands. We locked the house and went to the mall, playing nice music in the car.

At the mall we started at Mr. Price to buy my clothes because I think Mr. Price sells the best clothes ever! Thabo bought me everything I wanted there! He paid 1000 rand and something!

Then we went to "Shoprite" to buy groceries. When we were done we went to "Kentucky Fried Chicken." We bought six pieces of chicken, chips, and cold drinks and took it as a take away.

We were tired now and drove home and put our stuff inside the flat. When we were done we washed, made love, ate, and slept without wearing anything.

When we started to sleep we heard a knock at the door. Thabo quickly put on his shorts and vest and hid my underwear. I ran to the bathroom and listened. Thabo opened the door. He was shocked to see Thozama and a woman.

"Come in," said Thabo.

They greeted Thabo and asked "where is Portia?"

I was looking through the little hole in the door and locked the bathroom.

"She's in the bathroom," Thabo told them.

"My girl really likes water!" Thozama laughed.

Thabo nodded and offered them a place to sit and gave them biscuits and cold drinks. Thozama introduced Miriam to Thabo. I decided to pray in the bathroom.

'Dear God I'm happy to find my father but please give me strength to convince him to let me stay with Thabo.'

After I stopped praying, I did not say 'amen' and called Thabo. Thabo came.

"Bring my panties, dress and the shoes Thabo." He brought them. I put on my clothes and came out and sat down and greeted them.

CHAPTER 24

Run Away!

"**W**hy did you not come last night?" Thozama asked me.

I did not answer and just bit my nails.

"Answer your father with a smile on face," said Miriam.

I just looked at Thabo.

"Why's she looking at you?" asked Thozama.

I just took my small bag and checked to see if my cellphone was inside my bag and I stepped out of the flat. I started to run. I heard Thabo and Thozama calling me but I kept on running. When I was about to cross the road I saw a car. The car just stopped. Someone inside the car opened the car door.

"Get in," a guy said.

I did just that - I went in the car. No one asked me my name or introduced himself. There were three guys in the car. Two of the guys were talking too much. The driver was quiet. They drove to Bellville. I started to be scared and asked "where are you guys going?"

"We going to Pentech Technikon where we are staying," said the driver.

"Ok, but you must let me off here and I will catch the taxi to Cape Town," I Said.

"No, we are just going to change clothes then we will come back to town," the guy replied.

"Ok," I said.

I then took my phone out of my bag. When I checked my messages I was shocked to see that the phone battery was flat. I then made a silent prayer. The guy kept on driving until they arrived at Pentech.

"Come with us to our room. You must come with us to our room," they told me.

When I got in the room they offered me a chair. The room was very dirty and had no furniture.

The room only had blankets, a stove, dirty dishes, and clothes. I was waiting for them to change but they did not.

One of the guys sat next to me and tried to kiss me. I quickly stood up.

"What are you doing?" I said.

I quickly ran to the door, opened the door and ran! When I looked back the driver was running after me. I saw a room close by and started knocking, pushing, and kicking the door. Someone opened the door. It was a tall fat black lady. She was wearing reading glasses and a long dress.

I did not want to disturb this innocent lady.

"Sorry!" I said, pointing to the driver. The driver was running back to his room by then.

CHAPTER 25

Mandisa

The lady looked at the driver while he was running back to his room. She told me to come inside.

"I was busy studying. Where did you meet those boys?" the lady said.

"Sorry for disturbing you, but it's a long story my dear."

"Do you drink alcohol?" she said.

"No."

The lady then offered me a place to sit because I was standing next to the door.

"My name is Mandisa and yours?"

"Nice to meet you Mandisa, my name is Portia."

"Where you staying Portia?"

"I'm staying in town with my father. I have to go home before it's late. Can you please show me the taxi rank or the train station?" I said.

"I don't know why you knocked on my room door when you were in trouble, so for that I will take you home," said Mandisa.

"Do you have a car?" I said.

"Yes, I do."

I thanked her for offering to take me home. Mandisa told me to wait a minute. She wanted to pack her books. She packed her books then she took her car keys and locked the door to her room.

"I'm going to take you to town now," she said.

As Mandisa was taking me to Cape Town, I wished her luck on her test the next day.

"Be careful now and stop running around with those boys. Those boys were going rape you or maybe kill you. So from now on you must focus on your future," said Mandisa.

I did not want to tell Mandisa my story so I decided to agree to everything Mandisa said. When we arrived to town Mandisa wanted to take me inside the flat. She said she wanted to see if I was "safe." I agreed but I became worried because I lied about staying with my father.

When we arrived to Thabo's flat, I showed Mandisa the flat. Mandisa knocked and I stood behind Mandisa. Thabo opened the door. Mandisa greeted him and Thabo greeted back.

"I brought back this one," Mandisa said, pointing at me.

Thabo just went to me and gave me a big hug.

CHAPTER 26

Permission for Love

As we went inside the flat, I introduced Mandisa to Thabo. I told Thabo how Mandisa helped me. Thabo thanked Mandisa and gave her money for patrol. Mandisa thanked Thabo, said goodbye to me, and went to her home.

"Thozama said you can stay with me if you want to stay with me. He is not angry for you and you must call him when you arrived at home," Thabo told me.

I did not answer. I just took my phone and charged it. I bathed myself very nicely, lotioned my body, wore my night dress, ate, and layed down in the bed. Thabo layed next to me and played with my hair.

"I don't like what you have done today. Your father cried when you got into that car. We tried to follow it but we did not see where it turned because of the robots (stop lights). We tried to call you but your phone went into voicemail. I'm sorry for everything that has happened to you baby but I want you to call your father and tell him that you are safe Portia," said Thabo.

I just kissed Thabo and said, "sorry baby."

When I woke up, I took my phone and called Thozama. The phone rung once and Thozama picked up.

"My little girl, Portia," he said.

"Hi father," I said.

"Are you alright? Where are you?"

"I'm fine daddy and I'm in Thabo's place."

"Ok my child you can stay with Thabo but you must visit us and don't forget to come to Alma's memorial service on Friday at 10 o'clock in the morning."

I promised Thozama to come to the memorial service, we said our goodbyes and hung up the phone. I was happy now and slept peaceful that night.

Thursday morning Thabo went to his job. I woke up and prayed and thanked God for protecting me the day before. I asked God to make me focus on my studies and to help me have respect. I then made my bed, washed myself, cleaned the flat, and studied my books.

When I was done I cooked pasta for Thabo and watched the TV. Thabo came back from work and I dished up the food. We washed our hands and ate. When we finished I washed the dishes. Then we both washed ourselves, lotioned our bodies, and wore our sleeping clothes. We watched TV and went to sleep.

In the morning we woke up and prepared ourselves to go to Alma's memorial service. We both wore black and gold. Thabo was wearing a black suit, shoes, shirt, and a gold tie. I was wearing a black dress, shoes and my gold jewelry. I made my hair shine, combed my hair, and put on my makeup. After we were done we locked the flat and went to Gugulethu for Alma's memorial service.

CHAPTER 27

Jackie

There were many people there when we arrived at the memorial service. Thabo and I sat with the family. I saw my classmates and my teachers from the college but I did not have the chance to greet them because the priest was preaching.

During the memorial service Alma's coffin was in front next to the priest. There was a big photo of Alma. When the priest was done preaching, he asked friends of Alma to come in front and talk about Alma. No one was standing up so people were singing church songs until one beautiful lady stood up and the singing stopped.

"My name is Jackie and I'm a prostitute," the lady said.

People started to make noise and Miriam started to cry. I just held Miriam's hand. The priest told the people to keep quiet. The people then quieted down, looked at Jackie, and listened.

"I'm a prostitute because my father raped me when I was young. I ran away and stayed in the street until I decided to sell my body. I'm uneducated so that means I can't get a job. I met Alma on the road thinking she did not have a family. She was so young and beautiful and I asked her why she was a prostitute. She did not tell me the reason. I asked her to visit me but she did not. Now I'm standing here trying to convince you that not all the prostitutes are bad, so rest in peace Alma you will always be in my heart."

Jackie then went to her seat. The people start singing again. Then I remembered that Alma was my friend before I just stood up and went in front of the people. The people stopped singing.

"I'm Portia. Alma was my friend and she really loved me."

Then I looked at Alma's coffin and said, "Alma you no longer my friend you are my sister. I miss you Alma but rest in peace my friend and my sister. I will always love you."

Then I went straight to Thabo and cried.

CHAPTER 28

The Memorial Service

I realized that there were many people who were watching me so I decided to sit next to Thabo and be strong. Miriam was crying so painfully. The priest started to preach again. After he prayed and closed the memorial service, people went outside to wash their hands and went in the kitchen to take tea and biscuits and eat.

Thabo and I just went outside to wash our hands and went to Miriam and Thozama. We told them that we were going. Thozama hugged me and gave me 500 rand. Thozama told me and Thabo to go well. I thanked Thozama. Miriam did not say anything because she was crying.

Thabo and I went to our flat. When we arrived we washed ourselves, ate, and watched TV. We were quiet. I decided to go to the mall. I put on my makeup and took the 500 rand and told Thabo that I was going to the mall. Thabo said "ok."

I went to the mall. On the way I was just thinking about Alma and the way Miriam was crying. When I arrived at the mall I went to "Mr. Price" and bought a nice short white dress, white shoes, and white earrings. Then I went to another shop and bought myself a big chocolate and a cold drink.

I took small steps to Thabo's flat. When I arrived to the flat I found Thabo sleeping in a chair. I left him just like that and took the clothes I bought and put it in the wall drop. I then took a book and a pen and I wrote a letter for Alma.

"My dear sister who loved me while you did not know that I was your sister. I bought you that white dress and those white shoes I want you to wear them and be my angel. I want you to look after me. I will be something into this world just to make you to be proud of me. I will always love you from your sister Portia." I then put the letter in an envelope and put it on top of the fridge.

I then woke Thabo up and told him to go to sleep in the bed. Thabo went to the bed and slept. Then I took my chocolate and ate it, drank my cold

Mbali Madiki

drink with sleeping tablets and fell asleep in a chair.

CHAPTER 29

The Funeral

Saturday morning Thabo woke me up so that we could prepare ourselves for Alma's funeral. I asked "why I'm sleeping with my clothes on."

"You were sleeping in the chair my dear and I just picked you up and put you in the bed," said Thabo. We both laughed.

I woke up and prepared myself. Thabo was also preparing his self. We both wore black again. When we were done I took the "Mr. Price" plastic that had the dress, shoes, and earrings that I had bought for Alma the day before and took the letter on top of the fridge and put it in the plastic.

Thabo locked the flat and we went to the funeral. The funeral started at Alma's place. I was not sitting next to Thabo. I was in the room with the family. The other people were outside in the tent. Thabo was also in the tent with the other people in the tent. I was holding my "Mr. Price" plastic and really wanted to put the clothes in Alma's coffin.

The people from the mortuary brought Alma's coffin into the room where the family was. When I saw the coffin, I held Thozama's hand. All the people in the family were supposed to see Alma for the last time. The coffin was in the middle of the room. We all saw Alma and I was the last person, I was shocked to see Alma's face. She was so beautiful like someone who is sleeping. No one could notice if her head was cut because we could not see anything in the coffin. We could only see her face. Everything else was covered. The coffin did not have space to put the stuff in. So I took the stuff for Alma with me. I became worried but I did not give up.

When the viewing was done they took Alma's body to the grave yard. The family went in the black family car. Thabo followed with his car. Other people followed with a bus, while others were walking by foot singing.

In the graveyard all the people went to the place where Alma was going to be buried. The men were busy digging a big hole. The priest was busy preaching. When the men were done digging the hole, they took Alma's coffin and put it in the hole. The family was supposed to throw the sand first. There was a line to throw the sand. When it was my turn I opened my plastic and took the letter, shoes, dress, and earrings and threw them on top of Alma's coffin. Then I threw the sand.

CHAPTER 30

Saying Goodbye

All the people threw sand onto the coffin. When all the people finished throwing the sand, the men who were digging the hole threw too much sand on top of Alma's coffin. The men leveled the sand when they were done and put in the stones. They then put the cross in. On the cross was written Alma's age, name, and surname and "rest in peace."

The priest preached and closed with a prayer. The people went to Alma's place to wash their hands and eat. I was with the family. When I arrived at Alma's place I just washed my hands and drank a cold drink. When I went outside to look for Thabo, I found him standing next to the gate and looking worried. I tried to make Thabo smile by asking him to smile. Thabo did not smile. He just yawned and told me that he wanted to sleep.

I told him to wait there. I went to tell Thozama that we were going. Then I went inside and found Miriam sitting on a bed. When Miriam saw me she started crying again. I went to Miriam and hugged her.

"Thabo is tired and we are going now mommy. I will come and see you soon."

Miriam just nodded and kissed me. I then went to Thozama and looked him in the eye and hugged him. Then I left with Thabo and we went to the flat. When we arrived we both washed and wore our comfortable clothes. Thabo went to sleep. I cleaned the flat, cooked delicious food, and went to the bathroom. I locked the bathroom door and prayed aloud.

"Dear God, I have no one except you. Please God make me smile, make me happy like the other people, make me to focus at school, make Thabo to be with me forever, make me find another friend, and make me pass all my subjects! Amen."

Then I went to the kitchen washed my hands, dished up, woke up Thabo, and we ate. When I was done eating I went to the bathroom and washed my mouth and went to bed. Thabo washed the dishes and washed his mouth and layed down next to me. He kissed my forehead.

"You cook nice baby," he said.

I just smiled and Thabo played with my hair until I fell asleep.

CHAPTER 31

Going to Church

Sunday morning I woke up early in the morning. I washed myself nicely, brushed my teeth, lotioned my body, and put on my white dress, white shoes, jewelry, and make up. I combed my hair and woke Thabo up.

I told him that I was going to the church. He just nodded.

"I will be home later," I said.

I then took 100 rand from Thabo's wallet, took my cellphone and put it in my pack. I kissed Thabo and left. Thabo locked the flat and slept.

I went to the taxi rank and caught a taxi to Khayelitsha. When I arrived at Khayelitsha I went to my church. At the church Elizabeth's friends were happy to see me. They were telling me that they could not believe it and that I was "so beautiful." I did not say anything. I just smiled and concentrated on the priest. Church took only one hour.

When the church closed I went to the taxis and caught a taxi going to Gugulethu. When I arrived at Gugulethu I went to Thozama's house. I found my two brothers sitting outside with their heads shaved. I greeted them. They greeted back and started laughing at me.

"Thozama is also going to cut your hair!" they said.

I started thinking about how Xhosa people cut their hair when a member of the family died. When I got inside the house I found Miriam cooking in the kitchen. I greeted her and she greeted me back. She hugged me and told me to be free and do anything I wanted in the house. I smiled, opened the fridge, and poured myself a drink.

Miriam quickly dished up for me to eat.

"Where is your father?" she asked me.

Thozama heard me and said "I'm coming my baby."

Miriam laughed when Thozama came in the room with a razor.

"Portia take the towel and put it in your shoulder. I'm going to shave your hair," he said.

When I started to stand up Miriam said, "no one is going to make my baby girl ugly."

I smiled and looked at Miriam. Miriam then gave Thozama a pair of scissors.

"Take the scissors and cut nothing on top of Portia's head. Then the culture will be finished," she said.

Thozama did as Miriam told him. When he was done I finished my food. After I finished eating Miriam went to Alma's room and came back with two big bags.

"These are Alma's clothes and I want you to have them Portia," Miriam said.

I did not want to but Thozama whispered to me looking me in my eyes.

"Please take them. You going to make Miriam happy. Please my baby," he said.

I agreed to take the clothes and hugged Miriam. Thozama took me to Thabo's flat. Thabo was shocked to see those bags. I explained everything to Thabo.

CHAPTER 32

Finishing School –
A New Beginning

I did not find a friend again at the college. I was just talking with all the people at school and I studied very hard and finished my studies. But the problem was that I was only qualified to be an assistant social worker, assistant nurse, or assistant grade school teacher.

Thozama was supporting me nicely. Miriam was treating me like her own daughter and my two brothers were treating me like a princess. I was so happy with Thabo and still staying with him.

At the end of December I went to Vredendal to study there because Eric was calling me a lot. He told me when I was in Cape Town to come to study at Vredendal. I decided to go to get a bursary and promised Thabo, Thozama, and my two brothers that I was gonna come and see them during holidays. They promised to send me money every week.

I was worried about leaving Thabo and Thozama, but I had no choice because I was missing Eric, Elizabeth, Julia and Patricia.

I was ready for a new beginning.

About the Author

Mbali Madaki writes socially conscious stories from her own unique perspective, as well as the perspectives of others.

Stormy Skies is her first formalized book. She is currently working on her next book that is part of a series.

Stormy Skies

Mbali Madiki

↑UPTOWN
MEDIA - JOINT VENTURES

www.ingramcontent.com/pod-product-compliance
Lightning Source LLC
Chambersburg PA
CBHW061744020426
42331CB00006B/1351